OUR AMAZING WORLD

SNAKES

Kay de Silva

Aurora

Contents

A Gold-ringed Cat Snake coiling itself around a tree trunk.

SNAKES

Snakes are reptiles. They evolved from their lizard ancestors 100 million years ago. This makes them as old as dinosaurs.

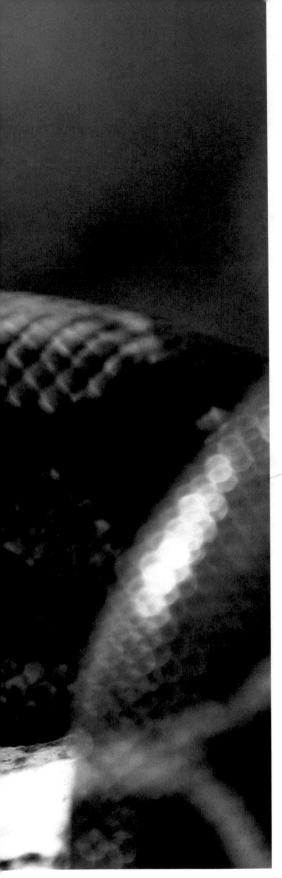

ANATOMY

Like other reptiles such as lizards, crocodiles, alligators, and turtles, snakes are vertebrates. Vertebrates are animals with backbones. Snakes' backbones are made up of vertebrae, to which ribs are attached.

A human backbone is made up of 33 vertebrae and 24 ribs. Snakes have 200-400 vertebrae and as many ribs. This helps them move and makes them very flexible.

Snakes' throats take up a third of their bodies. They have very long stomachs. Their throats and stomachs can stretch to the size of whatever they swallow. Snakes, unlike other reptiles, do not have legs, eye lids, and visible ear openings.

A close-up of a Boa Constrictor.

HABITAT

Snakes are found almost all over the world. They live on the ground, in trees, and in water. The only place snakes cannot survive is where the ground stays frozen all year round, so there are no snakes in Antarctica or north of the Arctic Circle.

Like all reptiles, snakes are cold-blooded, so their body temperature changes to match the temperature of their surroundings. This is why reptiles sunbathe to raise their body temperature. They also crawl into the shade to lower their temperature.

Snakes that live in cold climates save body heat and fat by sleeping through the winter. This is called *hibernation*. They find a cave or burrow and fall into a deep sleep until the weather warms up again.

A juvenile Amazon Tree Boa climbing a bush in the Equadorian Amazon.

A Northern Cat-eyed Snake using its tongue to smell its surroundings.

SENSES

Most snakes have poor eyesight, so they rely on their sense of smell and touch to escape danger, to hunt, and to find mates.

Humans use their noses to breathe and smell. Snakes use their nostrils to breathe, but they use their tongues to smell. Snakes flick out their tongues through a small notch in their lips. Each time they do this they smell the environment.

Snakes use their sense of touch to feel vibrations along the ground. They use this information to learn the size of their prey or food. They also use this sense to learn if they are in danger. Some snakes can also sense the heat from approaching warm-blooded animals.

A Bull Snake in defensive posture getting ready to strike.

MOVEMENT

Snakes do not have limbs. They use their ribs connected to muscles and their large belly scales to do the *walking*.

Snakes usually push themselves off a surface and slither along in a wavy motion. Some snakes, such as *Sidewinder Rattlesnakes* that live in the North American desert, coil to form a loop and hop on the dunes. This stops these snakes from being burned by the hot desert sands.

MOLTING

Snakes are known for their scaly, colourful skins. Their skins help them to *camouflage* or blend with their environments.

Their skins are made up of smooth scales. From time to time snakes shed their outer skin. This is called *molting*. Some people believe that snakes outgrow their skin. This is not correct. The reason a snake molts is to remove dirt and insects gathered as it crawls along.

A Common Garter Snake molting in the grass.

A sneaky snake in the grass dripping venom.

JAWS & FANGS

Snakes' jaws are not connected. This is so they can swallow prey many times as large as their heads.

Snakes usually have four rows of teeth on their top jaw. They have two rows on the bottom. Only poisonous or venomous snakes have fangs. Fangs are sharp teeth that are connected sacs in snakes' heads.

The sacs produce *venom*. Venom is a poisonous liquid found in some animals such as snakes, spiders, and scorpions. When venomous snakes bite, they release venom. In this way they kill or paralyse their prey.

A Boa Constrictor gobbling up its lunch.

FEEDING

Different snakes enjoy different kinds of food or prey. Frogs are the favorite meal of *Northern Banded Water Snakes*. On the other hand, *Queen Snakes* love crayfish.

Once snakes find their prey, they use their fangs to release venom into their victims' bodies. Their prey goes into shock or is killed on the spot. Other snakes, such as *Pythons*, use their bodies to crush or *constrict* their prey. Once the prey is still, they slowly swallow it.

Snakes do not chew their food, but swallow their food whole. When eating, snakes can only have one prey at a time. They do not need another meal for a while, as it gives their bodies time to digest what they swallowed.

A Californian King Snake ready to attack.

DEFENSE

Snakes protect themselves from predators in many ways. Snakes can use venom to kill their *predators*.

They also use venom to blind large animals that may threaten them. *Spitting Cobras*, for example, spray venom at attackers to protect themselves.

Snakes also rely on the vibrations they feel from the ground as a signal that they need to move to safer places.

A ball of Garter Snakes celebrating at springtime.

SNAKE BALLS

Some types of snakes form *Snake Balls*. This strange behavior happens in spring, as snakes come out after hibernation.

As female snakes glide by, hundreds of males gather around the females to form a ball. The snakes do not fight. It is said that this ball helps to keep the females warm and safe from predators. The females then chooses one male as their mate.

A Python hatchling emerging from an egg.

BABY SNAKES

Some snakes hatch from eggs. Others grow inside their mothers. Snakes usually lay eggs in a warm, safe place and leave. Unlike chickens' eggs, these eggs are tough and leathery.

Snakes such as the *King Cobras* and Pythons guard their eggs until they hatch. This is called *brooding*. Then the *hatchlings* are left to look after themselves.

Some snakes give birth to live babies. Newborns are known as *snakelets* or *neonates*. When they are born they are covered in a thin skin or membrane. Both the hatchlings and neonates use an egg tooth to rip open the egg or membrane and wriggle out. Snakes lose this tooth a short time after hatching.

A close-up of a giant Green Anaconda in the Peruvian Amazon.

ANACONDAS

Anacondas are found in South American rainforests and wetlands. They can grow up to 30 feet (10 meters) in length. This is as long as a school bus. Anacondas are excellent swimmers.

Their eyes and nostrils are located on top of their heads. This enables them to remain hidden underwater as they wait for their prey. Their prey includes wild boar, deer, birds, turtles, jaguars, and caimans (a small alligator-like animal). After a big meal they wait for many months before they hunt again.

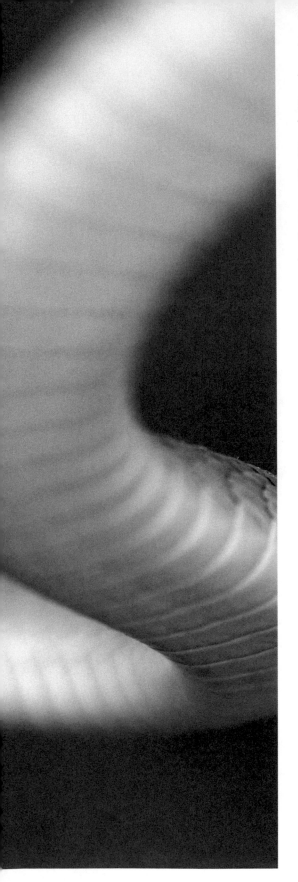

BLACK MAMBAS

Black Mambas are really gray and not black. They are the fastest moving legless animal on land. They can move as fast as 12 mph (miles per hour). This is faster than humans can run.

Black Mambas are the largest venomous snake in Africa. They hunt on the ground and in trees. Their prey includes bats, rats, birds, and lizards.

A deadly Black Mamba on the prowl in South Africa.

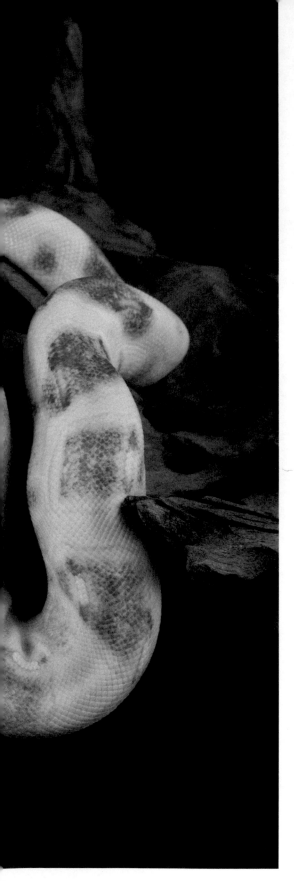

BOA CONSTRICTORS

Boa Constrictors are found in Central and South America. They live in forests and deserts. They are not poisonous. They are constrictors, so they kill their prey by squeezing and suffocating.

Their prey includes mammals and birds. They swallow their prey whole. They can digest almost anything except fur, feathers, and claws.

A shot of a rare albino Boa Constrictor.

A Cobra with its hood up in a defensive posture.

COBRAS

Cobras are found in hot tropical climates such as South Asia, Africa, and the Philippines. There are about 270 species of Cobras. Cobras are known for their hood.

They raise their heads and spread out their hoods when they are threatened or angry. This is to frighten predators. The hoods are made of flaps of skin. These flaps are connected to long ribs behind their heads.

Cobras may live for over 20 years. Their diets include rodents, birds, lizards, and other snakes.

A beautiful Corn Snake climbing the bark of a tree.

CORN SNAKES

Corn Snakes are found across the Central and Southeastern United States. Their gentle nature, reluctance to bite, and ease of care make them popular pets. In the wild they may live up to 8 years. As pets they may live for over 20 years.

Young Corn Snakes eat tree frogs and lizards. Adults' prey is larger and includes mice, rats, bats, and birds. These snakes are constrictors, so they squeeze tight to suffocate their prey and then swallow it whole, head first. Some Corn Snakes have been seen swallowing live prey.

A Plains Garter Snake sunbathing on a river bank.

GARTER SNAKES

Garter Snakes are found in cold climates, including Canada and the Central United States. Since they live in colder climates, they hibernate in winter. Hundreds of snakes usually gather together in dens. In Manitoba, Canada, some snakes travel over 20 miles (32 km) to their winter dens. This is one of the world's largest Garter gatherings.

Garter Snakes are small, so they have lots of enemies. These include raccoons, skunks, bears, and birds. Garter Snakes eat tadpoles, frogs, fish, and earthworms.

The Inland Taipan, also known as the "Fierce Snake," is the deadliest snake on earth.

INLAND TAIPANS

The *Inland Taipans* are known as the most venomous snakes in the world. They are found in the hot areas of Australia. They grow to over 8 feet (2.5 meters) in length.

These snakes move in on their prey quickly, strike swiftly, and wait for the poison to work. Then they swallow their prey. Taipans eat mice, lizards, birds, and small marsupials.

PYTHONS

Pythons live in Asia and Africa. They are found close to the equator, where it is hot and wet. They usually make their homes in trees or caves.

Pythons are constrictors that feed on animals such as monkeys, antelope, lizards, and caimans. Pythons need to eat only 4 or 5 times a year.

A Burmese Python gently winding down a tree in the Everglades.

RATTLESNAKES

Rattlesnakes live in the Western Hemisphere. They make their home in mountains, deserts, and plains. There are over 24 species of Rattlesnakes; they all have the infamous rattle.

Rattles are found at the tips of their tails. Baby Rattlesnakes are born with a *pre-button*. When they molt they lose this piece. After every molt a new button or segment is added. Unlike babies' rattles, the insides of snakes' rattles are hollow. The sound is made when the segments of the rattle bang together.

Rattlesnakes prey on small animals, including birds and rodents.

A Southern Pacific Rattlesnake shaking its ominous rattle.

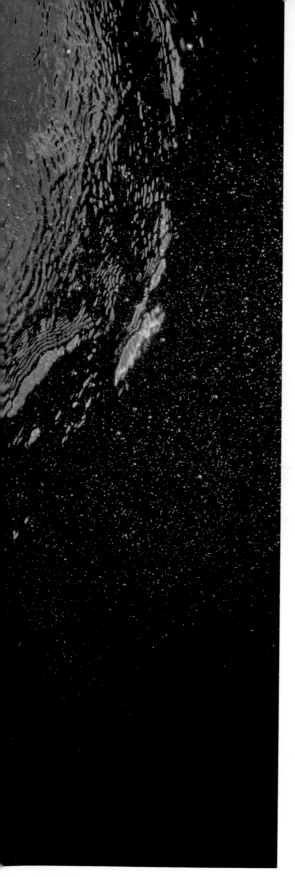

SEA SNAKES

Sea Snakes live in the shallow waters of the Indian Ocean and warm areas of the Pacific Ocean. All snakes can swim. Sea Snakes however, live mostly in water. They float up to the surface every hour to breathe.

Sea Snakes are poisonous. The most poisonous are the Beaded Sea Snakes. Three drops of their venom can kill 8 people! They will not bite unless threatened. Their favorite foods are eggs, fish, and eels.

A Sea Snake surfacing for air.

An endangered Emerald Tree Boa in the Bolivian rainforest at night.

SNAKES IN DANGER

Humans fear snakes, although most snakes are harmless. Others will harm only if they feel threatened. Sadly, today many species of snakes are endangered.

Snakes are a necessary part of a healthy environment. They are especially important in farming. Rats and other small creatures kill crops. Snakes keep their numbers under control. We must understand and respect the role of every animal in our eco-system. Protecting animals and their habitats is the key to our survival.

OUR AMAZING WORLD

COLLECT THEM ALL

WWW.OURAMAZINGWORLDBOOKS.COM

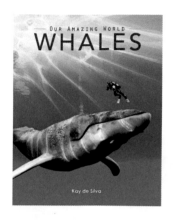

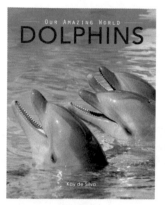

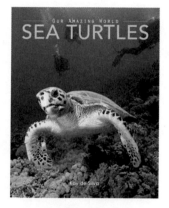

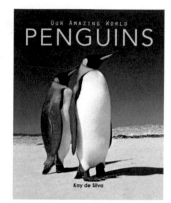

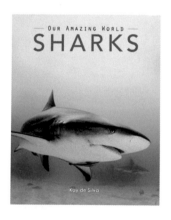

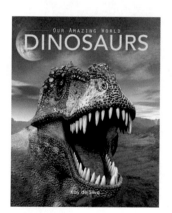

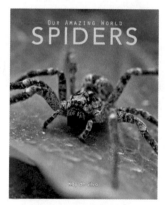

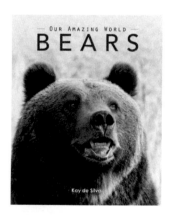

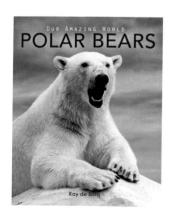

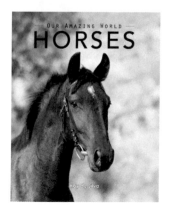

Aurora
An imprint of CKTY Publishing Solutions

www.ouramazingworldbooks.com

Made in United States
Orlando, FL
22 August 2022